C000117749

# AYLESBURY
# PAST & PRESENT

SUTTON PUBLISHING LIMITED

The busy Wednesday market, Market Square, *c.* 1907. Behind the clock tower, on the left, the Bell Hotel can be seen.

BRITAIN IN OLD PHOTOGRAPHS

# AYLESBURY
# PAST & PRESENT

KARL VAUGHAN

SUTTON PUBLISHING LIMITED

Sutton Publishing Limited
Phoenix Mill · Thrupp · Stroud
Gloucestershire · GL5 2BU

First published 1998

Copyright © Karl Vaughan, 1998

*Half-title page*: Kingsbury, *c.* 1910 (*see* p. 54).

*Title-page*: Market Square, 1953 (*see* p. 11).

**British Library Cataloguing in Publication Data**
A catalogue record for this book is available from the
British Library.

ISBN 0-7509-1770-9

Typeset in 10/12 Perpetua.
Typesetting and origination by
Sutton Publishing Limited.
Printed in Great Britain by
Ebenezer Baylis, Worcester.

Walton Road, *c.* 1900. The firemen seen here were part of the brigade maintained by Hazell, Watson &
Viney, printers. The pub in the background is the Old Millwrights' Arms.

# CONTENTS

Cambridge Street, 1939. All that remains of Webster & Cannon's building is the lowest few feet of the front wall which is now part of Sainsbury's car park. The neat lawn seen below belonged to Hazells Club which stood in Britannia Street.

A view of the town seen from Friars Square, *c.* 1968. The old Westminster Bank building next to Hilton's boot and shoe shop had just been demolished. Just behind the clock tower the Bull's Head Hotel can be seen and is under scaffolding, which means that it too was being prepared for demolition.

# INTRODUCTION

The history of Aylesbury has been an interest of mine for about fifteen years. During that time I have read books and looked at old photographs with immense enthusiasm. The 1960s are particularly fascinating because that was the decade when many old buildings disappeared forever, ancient buildings like The Bull's Head Hotel in Market Square. Streets disappeared during those years too, including Silver Street, of which only a small part exists today. Friarage Road has replaced the old Oxford Road and many other thoroughfares have been widened and straightened to accommodate increasing traffic.

Of course the 1960s was not the first era that saw many changes in the town. The Victorian period also made its mark on Aylesbury. The middle of the Market Square was cleared in 1866, with the loss of many ancient buildings, and the clock tower was built there ten years later. The town has a fine collection of other Victorian buildings, too, such as the one that houses the Halifax in the Market Square and the Literary Institute in Temple Street, which is a Rothschild building.

Although the town has lost much of its character to the ravages of development, there is still much to be enjoyed, in particular St Mary's Square and the surrounding streets – still a delightful area of the town.

The object of this book is to show as closely as possible where the lost buildings of Aylesbury were situated. Some have been easier to put in context than others and it has not been possible to include roads like the old Friarage Road, Silver Street and Silver Lane which are now totally covered by Friars Square. These roads have been completely erased from existence as their natural gradients were dug away to create the level shopping centre that we see today.

The photographs used in this book have come from many different sources. Most have never been published before and it has been a joy to track down all these wonderful pictures and to be able to ensure they are seen by as many people as possible. The aerial shots particularly show exactly what was where in the past. I hope this book will bring back memories for the older generation, and stir the imagination of the young people of the town.

The old Friars Square, *c*. 1968. At the time the square was still being built and looked crisp and clean. The ramp and steps seen here led into the open-air market. If you were to stand in the same spot today you would be standing on the corner by Mothercare, looking towards Superdrug and Samuel's the jewellers.

# CHAPTER ONE

# FROM MARKET SQUARE TO GREAT WESTERN STREET

*Looking from Silver Street towards Walton Street, c. 1914. The Bell Hotel is on the left.*

The King's Head in Market Square, 1963. The rubble of Adams' tobacconists is in front of it. This is probably how it faced the square originally, with no buildings in front to obscure it from view.

It is a shame that new buildings obscure the King's Head because it can hardly be seen, tucked away in the background. The hotel is one of Aylesbury's finest old buildings and it is good to see it up and running again after several years' closure.

Market Square, 1930s. The Crown Hotel is in the centre of the picture; in 1826 it was halved in size when the High Street (then called New Road) was built. Before it was altered, this building would have fronted the Market Square just as the King's Head would also have done at one time. The Crown used to have gardens and a bowling green at the rear. The hotel was demolished shortly after this picture was taken.

The statue of John Hampden has now been moved a few yards from its original position. When it was moved, a new time capsule was placed inside the base to replace the one that was put there in 1912. Market House and Crown Buildings have replaced the Crown Hotel, although there was the Crown Tavern at the rear of these buildings up until the 1970s.

Market Square, 1865. This is a fine shot showing the old Market House and other buildings in the square on a busy market day. On the left next to the County Hall is the Corn Exchange which had just been completed, having replaced the White Hart Hotel which was demolished in 1864. The Market House along with its surrounding buildings was demolished in 1866, leaving the square empty.

In 1876 the familiar tower was built, and incorporated into it was the clock that had previously been on the top of the Market House. After many years of being in the old Friars Square, the market has now rightfully returned to the site where it truly belongs.

A busy day in the Market Square, 1953. In the background are the shops of William McIlroy Ltd, ladies' outfitters, Foster Brothers, gentlemen's outfitters, and Home & Colonial tea stores. Photograph courtesy of the *Bucks Herald*.

There are now a lot fewer cars in the Market Square. The buildings in the background have been rebuilt, and after about ninety years in the square Foster's has closed.

The Bull's Head Hotel in Market Square after the demolition of the buildings in front of it, 1963. The timber-framed façade was a false one that was put up in the 1920s by the proprietor Mr Gargini. In 1968 the building began to develop cracks in the walls and had to be shored up. Sadly the structure was in such a bad condition that in July of that year it was decided to close the hotel altogether. It was demolished in 1969 and so another piece of Aylesbury's history was lost forever.

After the demolition of the Bull's Head, a new building which was to be called the New Bull's Head was planned for the site but this never came to be. For many years the site was used as a car park until 1980 when Hale Leys Shopping Centre was started. The centre opened in 1983.

Market Square, 1920s. The Green Man pub can be seen on the right with its fine balcony. Originally the pub was further up the square next to the Midland Bank. It moved to its more familiar site in the early nineteenth century. Next to Jones & Cocks on the left is Curry's which sold wireless sets and, as advertised on the side of the building, bicycles.

The shoe retailer of Freeman Hardy & Willis occupied the building on the left of the clock tower for many years. Butlers wine bar and restaurant has replaced the Green Man. The entrance to Friars Square is seen on the left.

The Market Square, *c.* 1950. This shows the fine Victorian building that replaced a pub called the Oxford Arms in the latter part of the nineteenth century. Note the different shapes of windows. In front of the Green Man is the entrance to the Grosvenor skating and dancehall, which was situated in a large building at the rear.

The large Victorian building is still there and is currently occupied by the Halifax. This corner of the square has hardly changed in the last hundred years.

The old White Hart Hotel in Market Square, *c.* 1864. It was built in 1814 and replaced an earlier timber-framed building. Photograph courtesy of the *Bucks Herald*.

In 1865 the Corn Exchange opened – a larger building than its predecessor on the site, the White Hart. It is now part of the County Courts.

Market Square, 1920s. The Bell Hotel had recently had another floor added and its front had been altered, a good example of a timber-framed building being hidden behind a more modern façade. The statue of Lord Chesham which was erected in 1910 dominates this picture.

Since the 1920s the Bell Hotel has had a large bay window added along the front of the building and the doorway that was on the corner is now just a window. The statue of Lord Chesham is now dwarfed by Friars Square behind.

Market Square showing the handsome Coach & Horses and Cross Keys pubs, 1964. The betting office of Racing Investors is on the left and T. M. Ashford, chemists, can just be seen on the far right.

Friars Square now occupies the site and looks rather bland in comparison, although it is an improvement on the old Friars Square which was ugly and out of date. The new square was opened in 1993.

Market Square showing the menswear shop of Weaver to Wearer, 1963. Just beyond the clock tower the Bull's Head Hotel can be seen (*see* p. 14). The twin lamppost shows that Great Western Street had already been widened by this time.

The Market Square presents a different scene today; it is largely a pedestrian-only zone with just buses and delivery vehicles allowed through. The Aylesbury Vale District Council offices now occupy part of the site of Weaver to Wearer and its adjacent buildings.

Silver Street, in 1963. This photograph was taken after the Greyhound pub, which used to stand on the left, was demolished to allow the widening of Great Western Street. At the top of the street is ironmongers Jones & Cocks, which has since moved to Rabans Lane. The Dark Lantern pub has expanded into the firm's old premises. With the Greyhound gone, there were three pubs left in Silver Street – the Coach & Horses, the Cross Keys and the Dark Lantern.

Silver Street is mostly gone now thanks to Friars Square. The Aylesbury Vale District Council offices are in the centre with the entrance to the Cloisters shopping area on the left. Friars Square is bounded by Market Square, Walton Street, Friarage Road and Bourbon Street.

Walton Street, viewed from Silver Street, 1963. Samuel's corner shop can be seen in the centre of the picture – a good place to get your newspaper on the way to the railway station. Behind Samuel's and the Victoria Wine Company were the garages of the Bell Hotel, which can be seen on the opposite side of the road.

The Bell Hotel is the only remaining building in this view; it now has the grubby-looking Friars Square facing it instead of the fine row of old buildings in the previous shot. The County Offices can be seen at the top of the picture with the entrance to Great Western Street on the right.

A fine view of Great Western Street, 1963. The shops seen here from left to right are Parminter's butchers, Tomkins' hairdressers and George Rayner, another butcher. Both Parminter's and George Rayner also had shops in Buckingham Street. At the end of this row on the far right is the Railway Hotel.

This is a perfect example of how to ruin a street which had a lot of character. This end of Great Western Street is now covered by this hideous tunnel where the bus station is situated. The other end of the street has been obliterated by the building of a subway and Safeway's car park.

The Railway Hotel, Great Western Street, 1963. This building was refronted and enlarged in 1898. It had a range of architectural features including gargoyles on the roof, some of which can now be seen on display in the museum. Friars Square is under construction on the left and the buildings that used to stand in front of the hotel can be seen on the next page.

It is a shame that such a fine hotel had to go in the development of Friars Square. It was among the last to be demolished as the new buildings rose around it. Nowadays anyone arriving from the railway station sees this concrete jungle as they make their way into town.

The fine late Victorian buildings in Great Western Street, 1965. The Railway Hotel can be seen through the trees with Friarage Terrace adjoining it behind. Opposite the hotel on the right of the picture is F.H. Sheffield funeral director, then M.G. Stanley plumbers and Kayes Linens.

Friarage Road now goes straight through the site of those Victorian buildings, although only a few years ago there was a roundabout here. The footbridge was part of the modernization of Friars Square and leads to the multi-storey car park.

Great Western Street, 1966, showing the newly built County Office block which looks very clean compared with its present appearance. The buildings on the left are part of Friarage Terrace which adjoined the Railway Hotel.

The County Offices can hardly be seen today behind the multi-storey car park, so much so that I had to stand back quite a distance from the original spot to get the whole view.

The County Offices under construction, 1965. The coal lorries of Timothy East Ltd are being loaded in the foreground. The station sign reads 'Aylesbury Town' to distinguish it from the other station which was in the High Street. The latter closed in 1953 and at the time of this picture the site was just waste ground.

The coal yard has gone and has been replaced by the main railway station car park. Many of the trees are the same ones as can be seen in the previous shot. They originally formed part of the gardens of the Old House, which stood in Walton Street.

The County Offices, from Aylesbury Town station, 1965. The massive crane used in the construction work was of a size rarely seen in the town before that time.

Now the multi-storey partly obscures the view of the County Offices. Even today the tower block provokes a mixed response from the public. As can be seen, the signal box has now gone; it is no longer needed as signalling is controlled from elsewhere.

# CHAPTER TWO

# AROUND WALTON &
# UP THE HIGH STREET

*Walton Street from the corner of Exchange Street, c. 1962.*

Walton Street, showing the original premises of Lucas & Co. furnishers, 1963. Lucas & Co. is now in Rabans Lane. The last building in this row on the left of the picture is the shop of E. Paragreen, leather merchants. These buildings were demolished in 1967.

After many years as the food department of Woolworths, the site is now occupied by Aylesbury Lending Library. This end of Walton Street has escaped being widened like the lower part, which is now a dual carriageway.

Walton Street, 1963. The poster board on the right says construction of the County Offices is in progress in the yard behind. The large building on the right with the white façade is The Old House which was built in the eighteenth century and at the time this photograph was taken, the building was used by the County Council. It was demolished in 1967.

Today Walton Street looks very different. The house on the left is virtually the only building that survives from those in the 1963 picture, although the cluster of buildings which includes Jackson's the bakers and the Ship Inn survives a little further up the road.

Walton Street at the junction of Exchange Street, 1965. In the centre of the picture is Kay's newsagents with the tiny old pub called the Bear next door. Jackson's bakery and the Ship Inn can be seen on the far right.

What a different scene it is today. The roundabout sits where the older buildings were and indicates just how many were demolished.

Walton Street, 1964. The old white building next to the Ship Inn is Mid Bucks Scooters. In records from the eighteenth century, the Ship Inn is listed as the Jolly Bargeman. A little further along the road is the newly built petrol station of Newtown Garage.

After only thirty years the garage has been demolished to be replaced by Old Brewery Close, named after Walton Brewery which originally stood on the site.

Walton Street, 1966. The new County Offices block is near completion on the left. The large building below it in the foreground is Walton Baptist chapel next door to Claude Rye's garage which sold both motorcycles and cars. On the opposite side of the road is the Ship Inn.

Today the road runs straighter and wider than it used to. In place of the Baptist chapel and the other buildings is the office block which is part of Equitable Life and is known locally as the 'Blue Leanie'.

Walton Street, 1962. The large building seen here is Walton Brewery. It was taken over by the Aylesbury Brewery Company in 1895. The buildings were demolished shortly after this photograph was taken. Further up the street on the same side is Holy Trinity church.

The entrance to Old Brewery Close is now on the left, while immediately surrounding it is land left empty by demolition of the garage that once stood there.

Walton Street where it joins Wendover Road, early 1960s. On the left is the Horse & Jockey pub, which is seen on the opposite page. Behind the pub is the turning for Walton Green and close by is the row of houses in Walton Place.

Today all the houses have been swept away and replaced by the gyratory system which is loved by many motorists. The large building in the distance belongs to Equitable Life. This is one of three on that side of Walton Street, the others being the 'Blue Leanie' (see p. 34) and its neighbour, a large square building which also has blue glass.

The Horse & Jockey pub, Wendover Road, early 1960s. This is one of Aylesbury's older pubs: it appears in eighteenth-century records and its history probably goes back further still. On the right is the entrance to Walton Green which is seen on the previous page.

Today the pub looks much the same as it did in the old photograph. In 1976 it ceased to be known as the Horse & Jockey and is now called The Aristocrat.

The corner of Wendover Road and Walton Road, 1968. This area is called Walton Grove and the main building seen here is the doctors' surgery.

The Midland Bank is on the site now with the police station behind it. What remains, though, are the two trees and the bench.

A quiet view of Wendover Road in Edwardian times showing what a narrow winding lane it was then. The Three Pigeons pub can be seen on the right.

Today the pub has been demolished to be replaced by houses and what was just a lane has turned into a busy main road.

Wendover Road, *c.* 1910. The large houses on the left were built in the 1880s. It must have been a quiet part of town then – not so now.

The Edwardian houses are still handsome today. The line of trees has gone because of road widening. Even today, with the constant use of cars, some people still use the bicycle as a mode of transport, though it is rather more hazardous than it was ninety years ago.

The Nestlé factory, High Street, 1962. This view includes some of the original factory buildings, some of which were built in 1870 for the Aylesbury Condensed Milk Company. The factory was enlarged in 1899 and Nestlé later took it over.

As with many buildings in the town, the factory has been replaced by a more modern version. The same tree remains, however, on the left of the picture.

The High Street, *c.* 1962. Parminter's, the butchers, also had shops in Buckingham Street and Great Western Street.

The roundabout and Dayla soft drinks (left) now occupy the site

The High Street, *c.* 1900. The Chandos Hotel is on the left while further up the street many of the houses were still in residential use and had front gardens – including the tall buildings in the centre with the row of chimneys.

This area is now dominated by office blocks, with Hampden House on the right and the former premises of Target Life Assurance on the left.

The High Street, after a heavy snowfall, 1963. The furniture and storage premises of Robinson & Son is on the left with Clarke's pottery and glass shop next door. George Tough, ladies' outfitter, is next to Clarke's and on the far right at the bottom is the Co-op store.

A new building exists where Robinson's was and on the ground floor is Iceland frozen food store; on the first floor is Blue Arrow employment agency, and above it is the Changing Room which is the latest health club to occupy the top floor. Half of the adjacent block was demolished to accommodate this new building.

The High Street, 1930s. The Gothic-looking building on the left is the post office and Universal Book Stores is next door to it.

Today most of the buildings in this view are new, including the one which houses the Woolwich building society on the right. McDonalds fast food restaurant now occupies the site where Universal Book Stores used to be.

The High Street, *c.* 1900. Longleys' the drapers can be seen on the left and next to it is the entrance to a row of houses called Winfield Row, the site of which is now occupied by Marks & Spencer. Opposite Longleys' is the Congregational church.

Today all that remains of the Congregational church is the tower which is just out of view on the right. It has since been converted into an office block; the rest of the church was demolished and replaced by Hale Leys Shopping Centre.

The High Street, 1962. The buildings shown from left to right are Narbeth & Co the drapers, F.W. Woolworth, Harry Hermon Partnership outfitters and, lastly, David Greig the grocer's. Woolworths was among the first firms to move into the newly built Friars Square in the late 1960s.

Narbeth's were on the same site until 1990 when a fire gutted the building. W H Smith has moved into the building previously occupied by Woolworths and has since expanded into what used to be Halford's cycle shop.

The High Street, 1962. Left to right: Importers Tea Stores, Spragg's baby linen shop, Jarvis's department store which occupied a large part of this side of the High Street, Eastman's dyers and cleaners, and the National Provincial Bank. The large building behind is part of Jarvis's newly extended shop.

Many of the small buildings in the previous shot have been demolished and larger ones now occupy the area. The tall building in the centre was put up by Jarvis's so it could expand even further. The original plan was to demolish all the buildings along this side as far as the Market Square and build a huge department store; thankfully only one part of it was completed.

Exchange Street, from the High Street end, 1967. On the right is the White Hart Hotel. Opposite the hotel is Highbridge Walk with the Ideal Benefit Society next to it.

Many buildings were demolished to allow the road to be widened and straightened. The building in the centre was formerly occupied by the Electricity Board and is now the County Council Planning Department; it does not face the street square on as it used to.

Exchange Street looking towards the High Street, 1962. The White Hart Hotel is in the foreground while at the end of the street is the large round gasometer that was part of the gasworks. The long building below it and the wall in front were part of the former railway.

The large office block called The Exchange now stretches along this side of the street. All traces of the railway have been obliterated by the new Vale Park Drive which follows roughly the same course as the old railway tracks.

The High Street end of Exchange Street, 1967. The White Hart Hotel can be seen on the left facing Highbridge Walk on the opposite side of the road.

It is hard to place exactly where the old buildings were with the new road that is there today. There is a bus shelter where someone's living room used to be! How things change.

Exchange Street after the demolition of The Old House which faced the entrance to the street, 1967. On the right is the old police station: the police have since moved to Wendover Road. The white buildings in the centre were the garages of the police station.

Exchange Street has almost tripled in width to include the area previously occupied by many of the buildings along Walton Street. The tall trees in the distance are those same ones that can be seen in the older photograph.

# CHAPTER THREE

# AROUND KINGSBURY &
# BUCKINGHAM STREET

*Harper's ornamental masons in Buckingham Street, 1963. The firm was next to Cooper's Yard.*

Kingsbury, late 1940s. The original bus station in this photograph continued here up until the 1960s when it was moved to its present site in Great Western Street. The Rockwood pub can be seen left of centre; at the time it was one of three pubs in Kingsbury, the others being The Red Lion and The Eagle.

This view of Kingsbury has hardly changed. The roof line through the trees has remained much the same. The Rockwood changed its name in the 1970s and is now known as the Lobster Pot.

The Red Lion, in Kingsbury, showing the central courtyard entrance, 1930s. This building is one of Aylesbury's few remaining ancient inns and is known to have existed as early as the sixteenth century. Other inns which have survived the passage of time are the White Swan in Walton Street, the Dark Lantern in Silver Street and the Queen's Head in Temple Square.

Today the pub goes under the name of the Hobgoblin and it was previously Mangrove Jack's. As can be seen, the central courtyard has been built over and now serves as the main entrance to the pub. However, the characteristic shape of the roof line, which shows the age of the building, has not changed.

Kingsbury, *c.* 1910. Seen here are Adams, stationers and tobacconist, and next door is Ivatts' shoe shop. Further down the road the sign of the Eagle pub can be seen.

Apart from the alteration in shop fronts, this row of buildings has remained much the same, although this photograph was taken shortly before work began on the two nearest buildings. At the moment the area is under development for flats and a restaurant.

*Kingsbury, Aylesbury.*

A rare view of Kingsbury, *c.* 1900. The large old building in the centre is The Angel Inn which stood on that spot for many centuries before its demolition in about 1920. Its ornate pub sign was saved from destruction and is now in the Victoria & Albert Museum, London.

The handsome building of Lloyds Bank has been expanded and has encroached upon the site of The Angel Inn. Beyond, the top of the County Offices can be seen.

George Street looking towards Temple Square, 1981. The old building in the centre of the picture is Curtis & Horn, agricultural engineers.

The old building has gone and this end of George Street is now a little wider although it is still one of Aylesbury's narrowest streets.

George Street, 1981. This view shows what a large area Curtis & Horn once occupied.

The site is now taken up by a large office block. Next to it on the left is the rear of the Queen's Head pub.

Looking down George Street from the Queen's Head end, 1962. The ground floor of the large building in the centre was occupied by bookmaker's, Jock Bezant, and on the first floor was the County Dancing School.

The old building was demolished in around 1979 and Regent House now stands on the site. High Society for Kids crèche has recently opened here.

Buckingham Street, 1963. Next to the Two Brewers pub is Sale Bros, grocers, then Rayner's, butchers, and Page's of Aylesbury, bakers.

Rycote Court and Bakery House have replaced the row of smaller stores. The timber-framed effect of Bakery House reflects how the old building looked. The ground floor is now occupied by the Barber Shop and Kall Kwik printing.

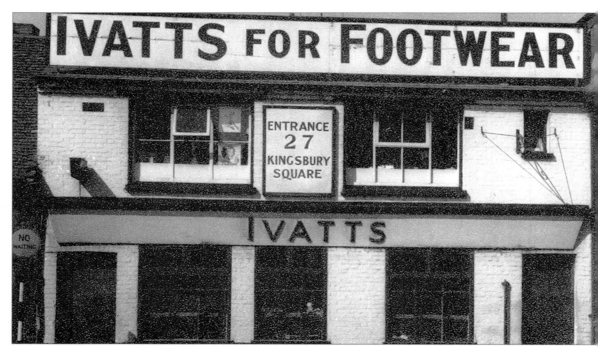

The rear of Ivatts' shoe shop, Buckingham Street, early 1960s. The family business started life in 1723 and remained in the front of this shop at 27 Kingsbury until 1983.

The estate agents Tony Nicholas now occupies the site, and is one of three estate agents at this end of Buckingham Street.

Buckingham Street, 1964. The corner shop of Lucas's newsagents was empty at the time. Between Lucas's and the rear of Ivatts' shoe shop is the Vale Driving School. Down the street in the large warehouse is Sketchley dyers and cleaners.

The buildings on the corner have now gone and the area looks rather unattractive. This part of Buckingham Street is one of the oldest of the town. Underneath the buildings in the centre of the picture in a large cellar is an old baker's oven and there are lots of little courtyards between the buildings. This photograph was taken shortly before the redevelopment of this corner.

Buckingham Street, *c.* 1910. The entrance to the Buckingham Arms is on the right. On a map of about 1800 the pub is marked as the Black Boy. On the opposite side of the road on the left is Hopcraft & Norris, brewers, and wine and spirit merchants.

The buildings on the right have been preserved but further down the street older buildings have been replaced by office blocks. The eye is immediately drawn to the big office block called Heron House in the centre of the picture; it is occupied by the JobCentre. It makes the other buildings seem small in comparison.

Buckingham Street, 1964. The white building in the centre is the insurance broker, G.W. Lay & Son, which moved over the road to the corner of Granville Street when these buildings were demolished in 1969. The firm has since moved again and is now situated in the village of Ashendon.

A car park is now on the site of the old Lay & Son building, and strangely part of the front wall of that building still remains on the corner of Coopers Yard. The front step can be seen where there is a small gap in the wall.

Coopers Yard, *c.* 1962. This view is taken from Buckingham Street looking towards New Street, where the rear of one of the houses can be seen. On the left is part of Harper's ornamental mason's yard.

A car park now occupies the site of Harper's yard and on the right is Heron House, where the JobCentre is located.

Buckingham Street 1962. This view shows the empty shop of Crooks butchers. To the left was Agro Electrical Co. which manufactured electrical accessories while, to the right of Crooks, part of the forecourt of Aylesbury Motor Co. can be seen.

The older buildings have been long forgotten now and have been replaced by New Bedford House. Litton House and Oakstead garage occupy the site where Aylesbury Motor Co. used to be.

The end of Buckingham Street with White Hill dipping away in the background, 1970. The building seen here is Fleet's newsagents and gents' hairdressers. It's a wonder they managed to cram so much into a small building!

The road now goes through the site of Fleet's and the telephone box has moved a few yards from its original location.

# CHAPTER FOUR

# FROM WHITE HILL TO RICKFORD'S HILL

*Cottages in the old Oxford Road with the entrance to White Hill on the left, c. 1910.*

Whitehall Street, 1961. At the time this was a quiet part of town and surrounded by just a handful of buildings.

Sunley House, occupied by the Social Security office, is on the site now and was built much further back from the road to accommodate another carriageway.

A quiet view of White Hill showing how narrow and winding it was, *c.* 1900. Just out of the picture on the left was a pub called the Seven Stars. Aylesbury ducks, like those seen here were commonplace in this area at the time. Duck rearing took place in farms around Aylesbury and eggs would be sold to breeders in the town who would keep birds in little pools in their gardens. They have been known to find their way inside the cottages too! The Aylesbury ducks had a rapid growth rate and were killed to be eaten after only eight weeks.

White Hill is no longer a narrow little lane. The road has probably tripled in width with the loss of more old buildings. On the right is the entrance to the car park of Big Hand Mo's pub.

Oxford Road, showing the quaint old cottages that stood at the bottom of White Hill, 1947. Next to the cottages is the original Hen & Chickens pub which can be seen on the opposite page. Photograph courtesy of the *Bucks Herald*.

It is roundabouts galore these days in Oxford Road. The only old buildings that remain are the ones on the right.

A lovely picture of the old Hen & Chickens pub in Oxford Road, 1963. By this time White Hill had already been redeveloped and Gatehouse Road was being built, as can be seen by the houses in the background – they were constructed in around 1960.

The Hen & Chickens was rebuilt further back from its original position and has only recently been renamed as Big Hand Mo's. The nearby roundabout system is still known as the Hen & Chickens.

Oxford Road, 1963. The Oxford Road Stores of G & I Fox, grocers, are in the centre of the picture. As can be seen on the left by the van, there were once a number of very old buildings on this road. Many were duck breeders' cottages.

It is a rather less interesting view today. With the construction of Friarage Road, sadly all the old buildings had to be demolished. Once gone, of course, they can never be replaced. The large buildings behind the fence are retirement flats in Prebendal Close.

Castle Street, 1963. On the left, between the two cottages and up a driveway is the premises of E. H. Oakley, weighing machine manufacturers. The white house nearest was formerly a pub called the White Lion which was one of many pubs in this street; others included the Plume of Feathers, the Black Horse and the Half Moon. Today they have all gone.

This end of Castle Street has been shortened a little which makes it even steeper than it was originally. All the buildings behind the brick wall on the right have disappeared to be replaced by a grassy area called the Mount. Oakley's has since moved to Rabans Lane and in its place now is R & A Electronics, TV and hi-fi repairs.

The Rising Sun, 1963. This pub was at the bottom of Castle Street and faced the old Oxford Road. The pub itself was not as large inside as its outward appearance would lead you to believe. This building has been photographed many times and it is clear how well it looked in this fine setting.

The dual carriageway of Friarage Road goes through the site now and no trace of the pub remains. The only buildings to link it with the old photograph are on the right. When the new road was built, the natural gradient at the bottom of Castle Street was cut into to make a flat, level road.

The corner of Mount Street and the old Oxford Road, *c*.1900. The building seen here is that of Joseph Gomm the butcher. It is hard now to imagine this area alive with farm animals. Photograph courtesy of the *Bucks Herald*.

This building is still recognizable today although there have been a few alterations. It is now converted into two flats and all the windows have been replaced, probably to keep out the noise of the traffic on Friarage Road which it faces. In Mount Street, round the corner, the white house has been through some changes; having had its top floor taken away, it has been shortened to become a two-storey building.

Oxford Road at the junction of Rickford's Hill, 1965. The Wheatsheaf pub is empty. Near the building is one of the new lampposts that were put in ready for the building of Friarage Road.

Today nothing remains of the pub. Once a quiet area, it is now busy with traffic thundering through here on Friarage Road which runs from Oxford Road to Walton Street.

Looking down Rickford's Hill, 1965. The Wheatsheaf, which is shown on the previous page, can be seen side on at the bottom of the hill.

Rickford's Hill is a little straighter than it was and where the Wheatsheaf pub formerly stood, there is now the road for Green End where the United Reformed church is situated.

Close to the top of Rickford's Hill, 1965. This handsome house was built in 1877. Just beyond it on the left is Friarscroft, which at the time was occupied by Aylesbury Municipal Offices.

Kidd Rapinet solicitors occupy a new building on the site of the house in the previous picture. The only thing that remains the same is the tree on the left, which was formerly in the garden of Friarscroft.

The Ex-Services Club in Friarage Passage, 1964. The club was formerly the Wesleyan chapel which had been built in 1837. In the nineteenth century there was a pub here called the Compasses, which stood in the foreground behind the wooden fence.

Friars Square is on the site now and looks much less interesting than the buildings which were there before. On the right of the picture is the edge of the Friarage.

The top of Friarage Passage, *c.* 1961. The wall on the right belonged to the former Methodist chapel which later became the Ex-Services Club, seen on the previous page. At the top between the old house and the Friarage is the rear of the public baths.

Today Friarage Passage is shorter and narrower. Friars Square now stands on the right and the Friarage still remains on the left. Bourbon Street can be seen through the gap at the top of the passage.

Bourbon Street, 1964. The fenced area on the right is the site of the public baths and at this time was used as a temporary car park. In the centre is Phoenix Assurance with Neale, ladies' hairdresser, next door.

The entrance to Friars Square shopping centre is on the site now, and just out of picture on the right are the offices of the local radio station, Mix 96.

Bourbon Street, 1964. This view shows how much more uniform the buildings are on the west side of the street compared to the opposite side. The small Victoria pub is clearly seen in the centre. Photograph courtesy of the *Bucks Herald*.

The building once occupied by the Victoria pub is now the Pound Shop. However, the bracket which held the pub sign has survived all the changes.

Bourbon Street on a busy day, 1947. The man with three crates in the centre of the picture is making a delivery to M.T. Cocks, grocer's and wine merchant's, which is on the far left. Next to it is the Tinder Box café. The public baths can be seen at the end of the street: they were among the first buildings to be demolished during the redevelopment of the 1960s. Photograph courtesy of the *Bucks Herald*.

Bourbon Street today. The cobbled road has been covered over and Friars Square has replaced all of the buildings on the east side of the street. The refurbished shopping centre does not fit in with the surrounding older buildings.

A rather unusual view of the corner of Temple Street and Bourbon Street, 1972. The building was declared a dangerous structure and had to be shored up to make it safe. Like many of the structures in this area, it later turned out to be an earlier building masked by a later façade. Photograph courtesy of the *Bucks Herald*.

The replacement building seems to have been designed to emulate what was there before. It must be noted that the previous building was there for about 400 years. Will the current one last as long?

Home & Hardware Stores, Market Street, 1967. This building suffered a similar fate to that of the Bull's Head Hotel in Market Square in that it apparently became structurally unsound. It was demolished the same year this photo was taken.

It is a great shame when a featureless square block is built in place of a building with such character and in such an old area of the town.

Temple Street, *c.* 1950. This is one of the few streets in Aylesbury which is still cobbled and has a fine collection of old buildings. The large building at the end of the street in Bourbon Street is M.T. Cocks, the grocer's.

The street has hardly changed at all; even the same windows are open in the Queen's Head! M.T. Cocks has disappeared at the end of the street along with countless other buildings, which were replaced by Friars Square. During the refurbishment of the shopping centre, between 1991 and 1993, it was possible to stand at the end of Temple Street and see the Bell Hotel through the exposed gaps, a view which had not been seen for about thirty years.

Temple Square, 1947. There seems to have been a bit of a parking problem on the day this photo was taken with ten vehicles parked where there should have been only four. On the left is E.P. Gilkes & Sons, builders and decorators. Photograph courtesy of the *Bucks Herald*.

Today the square looks much the same although strangely there are fewer cars parked than there were in 1947. It is good to see that these old buildings have been preserved: far too many have been swept away in the town.

# CHAPTER FIVE

# NEW STREET, CAMBRIDGE STREET & THE OLD RAILWAY

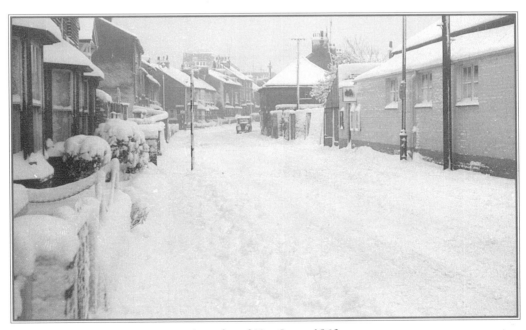

*A snowbound New Street, 1963.*

Bicester Road when the horse and cart was the main mode of transport, *c.* 1910. The wall of the Royal Bucks Hospital is on the far right.

Apart from the odd wall being replaced or removed and the apparent need for twin lampposts, Bicester Road has hardly changed at all.

Buckingham Road, when the photographer could safely stand in the middle of the street and take this picture, *c.* 1900.

Today many of the houses have been converted into flats while others, formerly private houses, are dentists' surgeries.

The junction of Buckingham Road and New Street, *c.* 1910. The Royal Bucks Hospital was built in 1832. On the right is the Primitive Methodist chapel.

This area now has a multiplicity of traffic islands and zebra crossings. You need eyes in the back of your head sometimes when negotiating your way through here! The hospital has been enlarged since the top picture was taken and, the wall has been taken back a few feet for road widening.

Looking down New Street from the Royal Bucks Hospital, 1960s. The large building on the right is the Primitive Methodist chapel. Just beyond the chapel is the sign for G.E. Lawrence, self-drive car hire centre. The tall building right at the end of the street is the telephone exchange.

With all the traffic going through here these days it is hard to imagine how it must have looked when the chapel was still here. All of the buildings along the south side of New Street have been pulled down to widen the road.

New Street looking towards the Royal Bucks Hospital, 1962. In the centre is the rear of the Primitive Methodist chapel which is seen on the previous page.

No trace of the old buildings exists today. A zebra crossing and traffic island occupy the site of the chapel.

This is Maldon Terrace in 1974. The road ran parallel to Cambridge Place which is off New Street. At the end of Maldon Terrace the rear of Baker's cycle and toy shop can be seen and in the centre of the picture is the large building which was part of Chamberlain's car engineers.

The view has now completely changed and the only building left to link it with the picture above is the rear of Baker's. Car parks now occupy the sites of the houses and gardens that once stood here.

New Street, 1980. Opposite the Oddfellows Arms at the end of the street is the Nag's Head which was part of the ancient district of Upper Hundreds. In eighteenth-century records the Nag's Head is called the Glaziers' Arms.

New Street has been widened to aid the flow of traffic and Upper Hundreds has vanished completely with the loss of many old buildings in that area.

Railway Street, 1972. The row of houses on the right was originally built as homes for the railwaymen who worked at the station near here. On the left is the Co-op store.

Car parks now occupy most of this street with only a handful of shops remaining on the left. The entrance to Hale Street is in the centre of the picture.

The Star Hotel in Railway Street, 1972. This was one of many coaching inns in the town. It was demolished in the same year.

This rather unattractive car park stands on the site today. In the background the new B&Q store can be seen.

Station Street, 1966. The handsome building in the foreground was the nineteenth-century Railway Tavern. With the finials on the roof, it was rather reminiscent of the style of the Railway Hotel that stood in Great Western Street. Behind the railings on the right are the remains of the cattle sidings of the old Aylesbury to Cheddington railway.

Only two of the original buildings are now left in Station Street and their days are numbered as this area will soon change again as there are plans to put a supermarket here.

Station Street looking in the opposite direction, 1964. On the immediate right is the Roman Catholic Hall and the yard with the white sign in the centre belongs to Aylesbury Tyre Supplies. Further down the street, the car is parked outside V.S.G. Bananas Ltd.

The car park now spans the bottom of Station Street. The Roman Catholic Hall still stands on the right but is now empty and awaiting demolition. Once full of buildings, this area is now mainly used for car parking.

Hale Street, looking towards Railway Street, 1974. The white buildings on the left are part of Aylesbury Turned Parts (True Screws) Ltd, based in Britannia Street.

Once again a car park has replaced old buildings. The brick structure nearest on the right, which is the Woolwich, is a recent addition.

The remains of the old Aylesbury to Cheddington railway from Lovers Walk next to Vale Park, early 1960s. The gasometer of Aylesbury Gas Company can be seen behind the telegraph pole and St Mary's church is just visible in the distance on the right.

The view is totally hidden today now that the large retail units have been built as part of Vale Retail Park. Gone are the days of hearing the whistle of steam engines in this area.

The old railway yards after the track had been taken up, 1964. This photograph shows how overgrown everything became.

Vale Park Drive now runs through where the railway tracks once were. On the left out of view are the units in Vale Retail Park, and in the centre is the new B & Q DIY store which opened in 1997.

Park Street at the junction of Stocklake, early 1960s. The line of the Aylesbury to Cheddington railway can still be seen after the crossing bridge was demolished and the rails were taken up.

Today just the line of trees remains, showing the original course of the railway which can still be traced between Aylesbury and Cheddington. The car showroom of NMC Citroën occupies part of the site of the old crossing bridge.

Alfred Rose Park with the buildings of Elmhurst Road in the distance, 1964. During the Second World War the field was ploughed up to grow corn and after 1945 Mr Rose, who owned the land, realized it was too damp to build houses on and he decided to make it into a park. Photograph courtesy of the *Bucks Herald*.

The trees have now grown and it is difficult to get the same view today. The field that was on the right of the park has now been built on and is covered by roads including Fairfax Crescent and Hilton Avenue. The park is still a pleasant place to be and is busy with squirrels in the autumn.

The Borough Arms at the corner of Park Street and Bierton Road, *c.* 1915. It was demolished in 1960. Photograph courtesy of the *Bucks Herald*.

The road has been widened and the pub has been rebuilt further back from its original position. It served as the Borough Arms up until 1987 when it became the Weavers.

Cambridge Street, early 1960s. The County Arms is seen here still with its original neighbouring houses to the right. The small white sign on the far right is of builders Webster & Cannon who had a yard behind these houses. Their main premises were next to the Odeon cinema. At the time they had a number of yards dotted around the town.

The pub is largely unchanged and the entrance to Cambridge Close is now where the houses were.

Cambridge Street, 1983. The building in the centre is in a rather sorry state. Just beyond is the telephone exchange.

The old building has gone to be replaced by a restaurant, Buona Pasta. One of the houses has been converted into the Locker clothing shop.

The Barleycorn, Cambridge Street, 1972. It is said that this building, with the former Harrow pub next door to the left and the Bacon Shop on the other side, was once part of the old farmhouse of the ancient manor farm of Aylesbury.

This end of Cambridge Street has not changed very much over the years and many of its old buildings survive. In the early 1980s the two pubs joined to become the Harrow and Barleycorn, but these days it is known as the Farmyard and Firkin – a rather less traditional name for a pub.

Cambridge Street, 1963. This view shows Saunders the grocers on the corner of Upper Hundreds: the building was in a bad state of repair at this time. The entrance to St John's Road is on the far left just by the last visible lamppost.

Much of this site today is occupied by the underpass which was completed in 1993 along with Upper Hundreds Way which is on the right of the picture. Behind the wall is the Royal Mail sorting office.

# CHAPTER SIX

# A BIRD'S-EYE VIEW

*The Royal Bucks Hospital and Buckingham Street area looking north, c. 1927.*

A nice view of the town taken from the Nestlé factory at the bottom of the High Street, 1963. To the right on the horizon St Mary's church can be seen, and just below it are the poplar trees that lined the Vale Park. The Victorian houses in the left foreground are those of Princes Road and Coronation Villas. Photograph courtesy of the *Bucks Herald*.

The County Offices dominate the horizon today although St Mary's church is still visible on the right. The poplar trees by Vale Park have gone and the new houses in Hilda Wharf are seen centre right.

Another view taken from the Nestlé factory, this time looking towards the Tring Road area, 1963. Immediately below is the distinctive factory clock and on both sides of Tring Road are the large factories of printers Hazell, Watson & Viney. Photograph courtesy of the *Bucks Herald*.

It was a sad day for Aylesbury when Hazell, Watson & Viney closed in 1997. Today Tesco's superstore occupies the site on one side of the road and on the other side is the Honda car dealer, D.C. Cook; the Kwik Fit tyre and exhaust centre is next door. In the foreground the Nestlé factory clock still stands proud.

The car park built on the upper part of the Recreation Ground, 1965. Just below the clump of trees on the left is the old town hall with the county hall next to it. To the left of the trees, part of the Borough Assembly Hall can be seen: it was the venue of many good concerts.

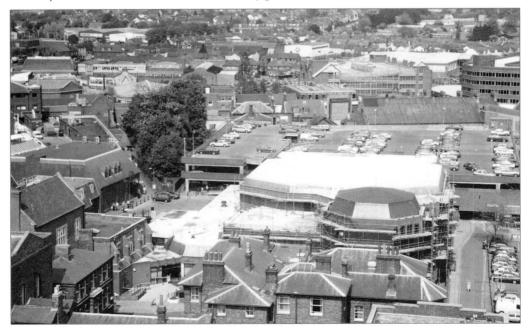

The Civic Centre dominates this view today; at the time this photograph was taken it was under scaffolding. The old town hall on the left has been halved and its roof has been flattened. Where the Borough Assembly Hall was, there is now Hale Leys Shopping Centre.

The canal basin area, 1966. At the bottom left is the timber yard of R.P. Richards & Co. Just above the centre of the picture, houses in the Queens Park area can be seen.

This view remains much the same, apart from Exchange Street at the bottom where the officers of the *Bucks Herald*, Wilkins Solicitors and Berkeley House now are. The canal basin is still full of barges and is a lovely place to walk on a warm, sunny day.

The High Wycombe railway line branching off with houses in Southcourt either side of it, 1962. The curving line of white houses is Nightingale Road.

This scene has not changed much at all. However, at the bottom of the picture the Brookside Clinic and the car park of Equitable Life are new additions. And the white signal box has gone from beside the railway line.

The railway station with Southcourt just beyond, 1967. Houses in Prebendal Avenue can be seen at the top of the picture.

A great deal of building work has gone on since the previous picture was taken. The multi-storey car park has been added at the bottom of the picture, while in the centre the large white factory of Schwartzkopf now appears. Also, a car park has been built over part of the railway track.

Friarage Road under construction, 1962. On the left at the bottom, the multi-storey car park is already in progress while opposite, on the right, the old buildings of the Railway Hotel and Friarage Terrace can be seen. The patch of land near the top was once part of the grounds of Aylesbury's fourteenth-century monastery.

Had this photo been taken in about 1990 it would be easier to relate it to the older picture because the roundabout was still there. Nowadays Friarage Road just breezes through uninterrupted. The roof of Friars Square is seen directly below and Safeway with its car park is just left of centre.

The town from the Royal Bucks Hospital, 1962. Right in the centre of the picture is a small old building, Fleet's newsagents, and behind is Aylesbury Motor Company. The large Victorian house on the left is Melrose House which stood next to the Primitive Methodist chapel.

Virtually all of the buildings seen in the old picture have been demolished and replaced by this huge expanse of road and roundabouts. As a pedestrian it seems to take an age to get from one side of the road to the other.

View down Buckingham Road from the Royal Bucks Hospital, 1962. Immediately below is the outpatients' department of the hospital. Dunsham Lane can be seen bending away from the main road. At this time it is still undeveloped and just a dirt track leading straight to Dunsham Farm.

Much of the view is now obscured by the new retirement flats on part of the site of the outpatients' department. Instead of leading to the farm, Dunsham Lane now stops at Elmhurst Road.

This aerial shot was taken in 1927. The Market Square can be seen on the left with Walton Street stretching diagonally along the bottom. The large, grassed area is the Recreation Ground and just below is the cattle market. In Walton Street the county offices have not yet been built and the buildings which stood on that site are still visible.

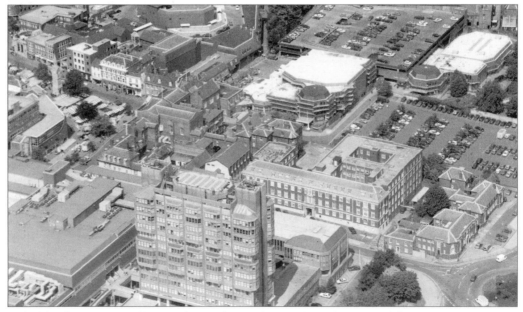

Both old and new county offices can be seen here and the cattle market is now full of cars. The Recreation Ground has mostly gone because the Civic Centre and Reg Maxwell swimming pools have been built over it.

Park Street and High Street area, 1927. The Nestlé factory is in the centre and the tall white building just above it is Walton Mill.

Walton Mill is now derelict and empty. Where fields once surrounded it there is now an industrial area. The Nestlé factory is still recognizable even though its chimney has been demolished and new buildings have been added.

# ACKNOWLEDGEMENTS

I would like thank the following people for their help and encouragement and for the use of the old photographs in this book: Peggy Sale, pp. 1, 19, 25, 28, 29, 31, 32, 33, 35, 36, 37, 38, 41, 42, 44, 47, 48, 49, 50, 51, 52, 53, 56, 60, 61, 62, 63, 65, 66, 67, 68, 70, 78, 79, 80, 81, 82, 84, 88, 91, 95, 96, 97, 99, 100, 101, 102, 103, 104, 105, 106, 109, 110, 111, 116, 117, 118, 119, 120, 121, 122; Mrs Englefield, pp. 10, 14, 20, 21, 22, 23, 24, 26, 27, 30, 34, 73, 74, 75, 76; the *Bucks Herald*, pp. 3, 9, 13, 16, 17, 69, 72, 77, 85, 86, 87, 90, 107, 108, 112, 114, 115; Richard Johnson, pp. 2, 4, 5, 6, 8, 11, 12, 15, 18, 39, 40, 43, 45, 46, 54, 55, 64, 57, 71, 89, 92, 93, 94; Ron Adams, pp. 58, 59, 98; Douglas Joss, pp. 113, 124, 125. All new photographs in this book were taken by me.

Thanks also go to the staff at Buckinghamshire County Council, the Royal Buckinghamshire Hospital, Adeco Alfred Marks, the Lounge, and Nestlé for letting me take photos from their buildings, and to Halton Flying Club for giving me the opportunity to take the new aerial shots on pages 122 and 123.

# BRITAIN IN OLD PHOTOGRAPHS

# SUTTON'S PHOTOGRAPHIC HISTORY OF TRANSPORT

To order any of these titles please telephone our distributor, Littlehampton Book Services on 01903 828800
For a catalogue of these and our other titles please ring Emma Leitch on 01453 731114